ITALIAN
for
Xenophobes®

Drew Launay

Oval Books

Published by Oval Books
335 Kennington Road
London SE11 4QE
United Kingdom

Telephone: +44 (0)20 7582 7123
Fax: +44 (0)20 7582 1022
E-mail: info@ovalbooks.com
Web site: www.ovalbooks.com

Language Consultants – Imogen Bright and Giovanna Bottazzi

Illustrator – Charles Hemming

Series Editor – Anne Tauté

Cover Designers – Jim Wire; Vicki Towers
Printer – Gopsons Papers Ltd.
Producer – Oval Projects Ltd.

Xenophobe's® is a Registered Trademark.

The Xenophobe's® Guide to The Italians
makes the perfect companion to this
Xenophobe's® Lingo Learner.

ISBN-13: 978-1-903096-18-5
ISBN-10: 1-903096-18-9

Contents

Introduction

When abroad you have to expect foreigners. Most of these foreigners will not speak English. Worse, to them, you are the foreigner.

This phrase book is to help you overcome such a setback and cope with the unexpected difficulties that may arise should you need to communicate with the natives.

Phrases are given in English. Then Italian in italics. Then the pronunciation for the English tongue is set out in bold type.

With Italian, enunciation is more important than speed. The more emphasis you give to what you say, the more likely you will be to convince the natives that what they are hearing is in fact their own language.

Pronunciation

Italian is a romantic, poetic, melodic language and you should sing along with the vowels. For example, a word like *matrimoniale* (a room with a double bed) should not be stated, but chanted:

maaah treee moan eee ahhh lay.

In words where there is a letter with an accent, that vowel should be pronounced forcefully while the others should remain meek, e.g:

docilità (docile) = **doe chee lee tuh**

In short words the first vowel should be stressed and those that follow cut short, e.g:

opera (opera) = **ohhh pair ah**;
mio (my, mine) = **meee oh**

All other letters are pronounced as in English, but with a light lilt hinting at sensuality.

a on its own should be pronounced 'ah' as though marvelling at a work of art.

è should be uttered 'ay!' as though delighted at a tasty plate of spaghetti.

h does not get pronounced, e.g., '*ho*' which means 'I have' sounds like 'o' – as in 'hot' or 'pot'.

gh is pronounced as though the 'h' does not exist as in 'ghoul'.

gn should not be pronounced as in the animal 'gnu' but as if it was just an 'n', e.g., 'knee' or 'knob'.

qu is pronounced 'coo'. For example: *que* = **coo ay**; *qua* = **coo ah**; *qui* = **coo ee**; *quo* = **coo oh**.

g before 'e' or 'i' is soft as in 'gin' or 'genuflect'; otherwise it is hard as in 'gun'.

c followed by 'e' and 'i' should be pronounced 'ch' as in 'cherry' or 'chips', but before any other letter, it is hard, as in 'cardinal'.

ch should be pronounced 'k', as in *chianti* = **key ant tea**.

sc followed by 'e' or 'i' sounds like 'sh', as in 'shut up', e.g., *scemo* = **shay moe**, which means idiot.

Of course, the Italian that is spoken in Lombardy is different to that spoken in Tuscany, Umbria or Campania, and the intonations heard in Rome are not the same as those heard in Venice or Bologna or Naples or Palermo. But this is just a colourful, regional matter because Italian is one of the less difficult languages to imitate, especially if you think 'comic opera' and high drama at the same time.

If it does not come naturally, forget about trying to sound Italian and go for sounding like someone who normally speaks English. This will not only simplify matters for you but will instantly prompt the natives to try and speak English to save you embarrassment, or, if they are male, to suggest they should give you instant private lessons. Thus, in a sentence such as:

Come, I would like to hear your heart beat under the Bridge of Sighs

Vieni, voglio ascoltare il battito del tuo cuore sotto il Ponte dei Sospiri

everybody will understand you without any trouble if you say it like this:

Vee ay knee, / vo lee oh / ass coll tar ray / eel / bat tea toe / del / too oh / coo awe ray / sot toe / eel / Pont ay / day / Soss pee ree.

3

The Alphabet   *L'Alfabeto*   **L'Alpha bet toe**

Within minutes of meeting you, Italians are likely to ask you for your personal details to meet later in the day. You should therefore be familiar with the sounds of individual letters to ensure they get it right:

A **ah**	H **ah ka**	M **em ay**	T **tea**
B **bee**	I **ee**	N **en eh**	U **ooh**
C **chee**	J **ee loongo**	O **oh**	V **vee**
D **dee**	K does not exist	P **pee**	W, X, Y do not
E **ay**	in the Italian	Q **coo**	exist in the Italian
F **effay**	alphabet	R **air ay**	alphabet
G **gee**	L **ellay**	S **essay**	Z **zayta**

Possible Pitfalls

In Italian male and female words are preceded by either *il* (**eel**) for male, or *la* (**lah**) for female. You should not worry unduly about mistaking one for the other as the Italians frequently do so themselves.

"How are you?" has two social conventions:

Formal, to a maiden aunt: *Come sta?* **Com may / star?**
Informal to old friends: *Come stai?* **Com may / sty?**

Goodbye has three social conventions:

Formal, to a new acquaintance:
Arrivederla **Ah ree vee dare la**

Informal, to a warmer friend:
Arrivederci **Ah reeve ah dare chee**

Positively chummy:
Ciao **Chee ow**

Discard Grammar

The Italians are forgiving and helpful about their language and will also want to show off whatever knowledge they have of English, so grammar is inessential unless you wish to write to the Pope asking for heavenly guidance.

Essential Words to Remember

Very nearly everything can be mimed. You can nod your head for 'yes'. Shake your head for 'no'. You can hold up fingers for numbers, and point rudely at anything you wish to indicate. You cannot, however, mime colours, the past, the present or the future.

If you lost a red mobile while visiting a church yesterday, you can convey lost by looking desperate, mobile by sticking your thumb in your ear and your little finger in front of your mouth, church by placing your hands together as though in prayer, but red and yesterday are tricky. The following should therefore be kept handy.

Black	*Nero*	**Nay roe**
White	*Bianco*	**Bee anne co**
Red	*Rosso*	**Ross so**
Orange	*Arancione*	**Aran chee oh knee**
Yellow	*Giallo*	**Shallow**
Green	*Verde*	**Vair day**
Blue	*Blu*	**Blue**
Violet	*Viola*	**Vee oh la**
Brown	*Marrone*	**Marrow knee**
Today	*Oggi*	**Odd gee**
Yesterday	*Ieri*	**Ee air ee**
Tomorrow	*Domani*	**Doe ma knee**
Now	*Adesso*	**Add esso**

To make a statement negative, put a firm 'no' in front of it:

No, that is not mine.
No, non è mio.
No, / non / ay / mee / oh.

Less Essential But Jolly Useful Words and Phrases

Yes   *Si*   **See**
No   *No*   **Noh**
Please   *Per favore*   **Pair / fav awe ray**
Thank you   *Grazie*   **Grart sea eh**
Many thanks   *Grazie mille*   **Grart sea / mee lay**
   (literally, a thousand thanks)

Good morning   *Buon giorno*   **Boo on / jaw no**
Good afternoon   *Buon giorno*   **Boo on / jaw no**
Good evening   *Buona sera*   **Boo on ah / say ra**
Good night   *Buona notte*   **Boo on ah / knot ay**

Don't mention it/You're welcome   *Prego*   **Pray go**

Excuse me (as in 'May I get past?')   *Scusi*   **Skoo zee**
Excuse me (as in 'I'm so sorry')   *Mi dispiace*   **Mee / dees pee ah chay**

Sod off.
Fan culo.
Fun / cool oh.

And (always an embarrassing one to mime):

Toilets
Servizi
Sair veet see

Small Talk

With Italians, there is no such thing as small talk. If you start chatting to someone you will be overwhelmed by the response to any simple statement or polite enquiry. For example if you suggest that:

It's a beautiful day.
E' una bellíssima giornata.
Ay / oon ah / belly see ma / jaw nah ta.

this will be agreed with, expanded on, then contradicted, then analysed in depth. So it's best not to start.

Numerals *Numeri* Noo may ree

One	*Uno/Una*	**Ooh no / ooh na**
Two	*Due*	**Doo ay**
Three	*Tre*	**Tray**
Four	*Quattro*	**Coo ah tro**
Five	*Cinque*	**Chink way**
Six	*Sei*	**Say ee**
Seven	*Sette*	**Set tea**
Eight	*Otto*	**Otto**
Nine	*Nove*	**No vay**
Ten	*Dieci*	**Dee ay chee**
Eleven	*Undici*	**Oon dee chee**
Twelve	*Dodici*	**Doe dee chee**
Thirteen	*Tredici*	**Tray dee chee**
Fourteen	*Quattordici*	**Coo ah tore dee chee**
Fifteen	*Quindici*	**Queen dee chee**
Sixteen	*Sedici*	**Said ee chee**
Seventeen	*Diciassette*	**Dee chee ah set ay**
Eighteen	*Diciotto*	**Dee chee otto**
Nineteen	*Diciannove*	**Dee cha no vay**
Twenty	*Venti*	**Vent tea**

Twenty One	*Ventuno*	**Vent too no**	
Twenty two	*Ventidue*	**Vent tea doo ay**	etc.
Thirty	*Trenta*	**Trent ah**	
Forty	*Quaranta*	**Coo ah run ta**	
Fifty	*Cinquanta*	**Chink coo ant ah**	
Sixty	*Sessanta*	**Say santa**	
Seventy	*Settanta*	**Say tan ta**	
Eighty	*Ottanta*	**Oh tan ta**	
Ninety	*Novanta*	**No van ta**	
One Hundred	*Cento*	**Chen toe**	
Two hundred	*Duecento*	**Doo ay chen toe**	etc.
One thousand	*Mille*	**Meal ay**	
Two thousand	*Due mila*	**Doo ay / meal ah**	
Three thousand	*Tremila*	**Tray / meal ah**	etc.
One hundred thousand	*Centomila*	**Chen toe meal ah**	
One million	*Un milione*	**Oon / meal lee oh nay**	
First	*Primo*	**Pree mo**	
Second	*Secondo*	**Say coon doe**	
Third	*Terzo*	**Tairts zo**	

Days of the Week (which have small letters)

Monday	*lunedì*	**loon ay dee**
Tuesday	*martedì*	**mart ay dee**
Wednesday	*mercoledì*	**mare co lay dee**
Thursday	*giovedì*	**jaw vay dee**
Friday	*venerdì*	**ven air dee**
Saturday	*sabato*	**sah bar toe**
Sunday	*domenica*	**doe men knee car**

A day *Un giorno* **Oon / jaw no**
Two days *Due giorni* **Doo ay / jaw knee**
A week *Una settimana* **Oon ah / settee ma na**
A fortnight *Due settimane* **Doo ay / settee ma nay**

8

Months *Mesi* Maisy

| One month | *Un mese* | **Oon / maze zay** |
| Two months | *Due mesi* | **Do ay / maisy** |

January	*Gennaio*	**Gen ah yo**
February	*Febbraio*	**Feb bra yo**
March	*Marzo*	**Mart zo**
April	*Aprile*	**Ah pree lay**
May	*Maggio*	**Mad jaw**
June	*Giugno*	**Jew knee oh**
July	*Luglio*	**Loo leo**
August	*Agosto*	**Ah goss toe**
September	*Settembre*	**Set em bray**
October	*Ottobre*	**Otto bray**
November	*Novembre*	**No vem bray**
December	*Dicembre*	**Dee chem bray**

| A year | *Un anno* | **Oon / ah no** |
| Two years | *Due anni* | **Doo ay / ah knee** |

Spring	*Primavera*	**Pree ma vair ah**
Summer	*Estate*	**Ay start ay**
Autumn	*Autunno*	**Ow too no**
Winter	*Inverno*	**In vair no**

Time *Ora* Aura

Five o'clock *Sono le cinque* **So no / lay / chink way**

Quarter past five *Sono le cinque e un quarto* **So no / lay / chink way / ay / oon / coo are toe**

Half past five *Sono le cinque e mezzo* **So no / lay / chink way / ay / mets so**

Quarter to six *Sono le sei meno un quarto* **So no / lay / say yee / men oh / oon / coo are toe**

9

The Family *La Famiglia* La / Fah meal lee ah

One of the most important institutions in Italy is the family, and loyalty to that family. It is imperative therefore that you know who is who when you venture into an acquaintance's circle:

Mother	*Madre*	**Ma dray**
Father	*Padre*	**Pa dray**
Daughter	*Figlia*	**Fee lee ah**
Son	*Figlio*	**Fee lee oh**
Sister	*Sorella*	**Sore ella**
Brother	*Fratello*	**Fra tell oh**
Aunt	*Zia*	**Zee ah**
Uncle	*Zio*	**Zee oh**
Cousin (male	*Cugino*	**Coo gee no**
Cousin (female)	*Cugina*	**Coo gee na**
Niece	*Nipote*	**Knee poe tay**
Nephew	*Nipote*	**Knee poe ta**
Wife	*Moglie*	**Molly ay**
Husband	*Marito*	**Marie toe**
Mother-in-law	*Suocera*	**Sue oh chair ah**
Father-in-law	*Suocero*	**Sue oh chair oh**
Sister-in-law	*Cognata*	**Con knee ah ta**
Brother-in-law	*Cognato*	**Con knee ah toe**
Son-in-law	*Genero*	**Gen air oh**
Daughter-in-law	*Nuora*	**Noo oar ah**
Grandmother	*Nonna*	**No na**
Grandfather	*Nonno*	**No no**
Grandchild	*Nipote*	**Knee poe tay**
Fiancé (female)	*Fidanzata*	**Fee dance ah ta**
Fiancé (male)	*Fidanzato*	**Fee dance ah toe**

Godfather   *Padrino* **Pa dree no**

Lover (female) *Innamorata* **In ah more ah ta**
  (male) *Innamorato* **In ah more ah toe**
or: (both sexes) *Amante* **Ah mun tay**

How do you do?
Come sta?
Com may / star?

It was nice to meet you.
E' stato un piacere conoscerla.
Ay / star toe / oon / pee ah chair ray / con oh share la.

Why does your mother look at me that way?
Perchè tua madre mi guarda in quel modo?
**Pair kay / too ah / mad ray / mee / goo are da / in / coo
ell / mo doe?**

Emergencies *Emergenze* **Emma gent say**

Help! *Aiuto!* **Eye yoo toe!**

There's been an accident.
C'è stato un incidente.
Chay / star toe / oon / in chee dent ay.

Call for a doctor.
Chiamate un dottore.
Key ah mah tay / oon / dot awe ray.

Call for an ambulance.
Chiamate un ambulanza.
Key ah ma tay / oon / am boo lanza.

Call for the police.
Chiamate la polizia.
Key ah mah tay / la / pol eat zee ah.

Call for a funeral director.
Chiamare un impresa funebre.
Key ah mah ray / oon / eem press ah / foo nay bray.

Are you all right?
Sta bene?
Sta / ben nay?

I am about to give birth – be sick – collapse.
Sto per partorire – vomitare – cadere.
Sto / pair / part or ree ray – vomit are ray – cad are ray.

I am allergic to aspirin – prawns – nitro glycerine.
Sono allergico all' aspirina – gamberi – nitroglycerine.
Sono / allergic oh / al / asp pee ree nah – gamb air ee – neat roe gliss air ree nay.

Please contact my relatives. Their address is in my pocket.
Per favore può contattare i miei familiari. Il loro indirizzo è in mia tasca.
Pair / favor ay / poo oh / con tat are ray / ee / mee ay ee / fam ee lee ah ree. / Eel / loro / indy ree zo / ay / in / mee ah / tasker.

I am with my best friend's wife. Please don't tell anybody.
Sto con la moglie del mio migliore amico. Per favore non lo dica a nessuno.
Sto / con / la / molly ay / del / mee oh / mee lee or ray / am eek oh. / Pair / fav awe ray / non / low / dicker / ah / nay soon oh.

At the Chemist *Alla Farmacia* Alla / Farmer chee ah

Chemists in Italy are patient friendly and medically knowl-edgeable. For minor problems consult them first.

What would you recommend for … ?
Che cosa raccomanda per … ?
Kay / cosa / rack command ah / pair … ?

Blisters	*Vesciche*	**Ves chee kay**
Insomnia	*Insonnia*	**In son knee ah**
Sunburn	*Bruciture solari*	**Broo chee ah tour / so la ray**
Piles	*Emorroidi*	**Em more roid dee**

Chronic Indigestion *Indigestione cronica* **Indy gest tea oh nay / crony car**

Menstruation pains *Dolori mestruali* **Doll awe ree / mess true ah lee**

Flatulence *Gonfiore di stomaco* **Gone fee oh ray / dee / stow mack oh**

13

I have a headache.
Ho mal di testa.
Oh / mal / dee / testa.

I have a fever.
Ho la febbre.
Oh / la / feb ray.

I feel dizzy.
Mi gira la testa.
Mee / gee rah / la / testa.

I have a cough – sore throat.
Ho la tosse – mal di gola.
Oh / la / toss ay – mal / dee / goal ah.

I am unbearably constipated.
Sono molto costipato.
So no / malt toe / coss tee pah toe.

I've got violent diarrhoea.
Ho una violenta diarrea.
Oh / oon ah / vee oh lent ah / dee ah ray ah.

At the Doctor *Dal Dottore* Dull / Dot awe ray

I have a serious – constant – spasmodic pain in the area of my:
Io ho un dolore serio – costante – spasmodico nella parte del mio:
Ee oh / oh / oon / doe law ray / sair ree oh – cost ant tay – spas mod dick oh / nella / part ay / del / mee oh: …

Ear	*Orecchio*	**Or wreck key oh**
Eye	*Occhio*	**Ock key oh**
Neck	*Collo*	**Coll low**
Shoulder	*Spalla*	**Spalla**

14

Back	*Schiena*	**Skee ay na**
Heart	*Cuore*	**Coo awe ray**
Chest	*Petto*	**Pet oh**
Arm	*Braccio*	**Bra chee oh**
Thigh	*Coscia*	**Coss chee ah**
Leg	*Gamba*	**Gamba**
Knee	*Ginocchio*	**Gee knock ee oh**
Foot	*Piede*	**Pee aid day**
Toe	*Dito del piede*	**Dee toe / del / pee aid day**
Rectum	*Retto*	**Ret toe**
Genitals	*Genitali*	**Jenny ta lee**

NB: If the painful area is not listed – point.

I have had stomach pains for the last week.
Ho avuto dolori di stomaco per una settimana.
Oh / av ooh toe / dol law ree / dee / stow mack oh / pair / oon ah / settee mah na.

My poo-poo is black; brown; beige; green.
Miei escrementi hanno un colore nero; marrone; beige; verde.
Mee ay ee / esk rem men tee / an oh / oon / col awe ray / nay roe; / marrow nay; / bay ee jay; / vair day.

I have been spitting blood.
Sto sputando sangue.
Sto / spoo tan doe / san goo ay.

I am accused of being a hypochondriac but I am sure I am suffering from idiopathic thrombocytopenic purpura.
Mi accusano di essere un ipocondriaco ma sono dicuro che soffro di idiopatetic trombocitopenic purpura.
Me / ah coos ah no / dee / es say ray / oon / ee po con dree ah co / ma / so no / dick coo roe / kay / soff roe / dee / idio pat tet tick / trombo see toe pen nick / poor poo ra.

15

I think I am going to die
Mi sento di morire.
Me / sento / dee / more rear ray.

At the Hospital *All'ospedale* **Al / oss pay dahl lay**

I am suffering terribly. Could I have morphine?
Sto soffrendo terribilmente. Mi può dare morfina?
**Stow / sof friend oh / tair ree bill men tay. / Mee / poo
oh / dah ray / morphine ah?**

That was nice. Could I have another shot?
Oh che bene. Mi può dare un'altra iniezione?
**Oh / kay / ben ay. / Mee / poo oh / dah ray / oon / ultra /
in nets zee oh nay?**

Nurse, I need a bedpan urgently.
Infermiera, ho urgentamente bisogno di una padella.
**In fair me air ah, / oh / urgent ah men tay / bee so knee
oh / dee / oon ah / pad ella.**

Could you give me another pillow?
Mi potrebbe dare un altro cuscino?
Me / pot ray bay / dah ray / oon / ultro / coo she no?

No, I do not want a blanket bath.
No, non voglio un asciugamano da bagno.
**No, / non / voe lee oh / oon / ah sugar mah no / da / ban
knee oh.**

I think there are fleas inside my plaster.
Penso che ci sono pulci dentro la mia ingessatura.
**Pen so / kay / chee / so no / pull chee / dent roe / la / mee
ah / in jess ah too rah.**

My mother in law is coming to visit me. Could you tell her I am in a coma.

Mia suocera mi viene a visitare. Le può dire che sono in coma?

Me ah / sue oh chair ah / mee / vee ay nay / ah / visit ah ray. / Lay / poo oh / dee ray / kay / so no / in / coma?

When can I leave?

Quando potrò uscire?

Coo an doe / pot roe / ooh she ray?

At the Dentist   *Dal Dentista*   Dahl / den tea star

I have unbearable toothache.

Ho mal dolor di denti terribile.

Oh / mull / dol law / dee / dent tea / terry bee lay.

I have lost a filling.

Ho perso la impiombatura.

Oh / pair so / la / eem pee om bat too rah.

My gums are sore.

La mie gengive sono irritate.

La / mee ay / gen jeeve ay / so no / ee ree tah tay.

That hurts!

Qui fa male!

Key / fa / ma lay!

Of course I want an anaesthetic.

Naturalemente voglio un anestetico.

Na too rah lament tay / voe lee oh / oon / an nest te teak oh.

Where do I spit?
Dove posso sputare?
Doe vay / posso / spoot are ay?

Should my tooth have come out like that?
Mi deve tirare il mio dente così?
Me / day vay / tee rah ray / il / mee oh / dent ay / cosy?

At the Optician *Dall'Ottico* Dahl / ot tick co

I have broken my spectacles. Can you replace them?
Ho rotto i miei occhiali. Me li può sostituirli?
Oh / rot oh / ee / me ay ee / ock key ah lee. / Me / lee / poo oh / sos tit too early?

I have lost one of my contact lenses. It fell into the minestrone and melted.
Ho perso una delle mie lenti a contatto. E' caduta nel minestrone e si è squaata.
Oh / pair so / ooh na / dell lay / mee ay / lent tea / ah / con tah toe. / Ay / cad doo ta / nell / mee knee strow nay / ay / see / ay / skoo ah lee ah ta.

I am myopic.
Sono miope.
So no / mee oh pay.

I am long sighted.
Vedo solo da lontano.
Ved oh / so no / ved oh / da / lon tah no.

What chart where?
Che graduazione?
Kay / gra doo ah zee oh nay?

Getting About *In Giro* In jee roe

On Foot *A piedi* Ah pee ay dee

Locals will give you directions with much gesticulation and volumes of words, so make your life simple and just ask:

Where is …? *Dov'è …?* **Doe vay …?**

To which you may get the answer:

Dree toe. *Dritto*. Straight on.

La / pro see ma / ah / dess tra.
La prossima a destra.
Next right.

La / pro see ma / ah / see knees tra.
La prossima a sinistra.
Next left.

La / seconda / ah / dess tra.
La seconda a destra.
Second right.

La / tairt za / ah / see knees tra.
La terza a sinistra.
Third left.

In dee a tro / da / coo ell / lato.
Indietro da quel lato.
Back that-a-way.

If you do not understand this because of rural accents, try:

Can you show me where that is on this map?
Mi può indicare dov'è sulla mappa?
Mee / poo oh / indi car ray / doe vay / ay / sue la / mappa?

Can you draw it on this piece of paper?
Lo può disegnare su questo pezzo di carta?
Low / poo oh / diz en yah ray / sue / coo ess toe / pets so / dee / carter?

Where can I get a taxi?
Dove posso prendere un taxi?
Doe vay / poo so / pren dare ray / oon / taxi?

By Taxi   *Con il Taxi*   Con / eel / Taxi

State your destination, e.g:

10, Bellini Street, Rome
Numero dieci Via Bellini, Roma
Noo may roe / dee ah chee / Vee ah / Bellini, / Rome ah

after which you should keep quiet and listen to the driver singing one or two of his favourite Puccini arias while he takes you by the longest route possible to wherever you don't want to go.

By Bus   *Per Autobus*   Pair / Ow toe boos

Where can I get a bus for Florence?
Dove posso prendere un autobus per Firenze?
Doe vay / posso / pren dare ray / oon / ow toe boos / pair / Fee ren zay?

Does this stop near the statue of Michelangelo's David?
Si ferma vicino alla statua di Davide di Michelangelo?
See / fair ma / vee chee no / ah la / stat too ah / dee / Dah veed day / dee / Mee kell anne jello?

Could you tell me where I get off?
Mi può dire dove scendere?
Mee / poo oh / dee ray / doe vay / shh end ah ray?

How long does it take to get there?
Quanto tempo impiega per andarci?
Coo an toe / tempo / eem pee ay ya / pair / and arch ee?

I was told this bus goes to Florence.
Mi appena detto che questo autobus andava a Firenze.
Me / ah no / ah pen ah / debt toe / kay / coo es toe / ow toe bus / and ah va / ah / Fee wren zee.

I am on the wrong bus. Please stop, I want to get off.
Sono sull'autobus sbagliato. Può fermare per favore, voglio scendere.
Sono / sue low toe boos / sbah lee ah toe. / Poo oh / fair ma ray / pair / fav awe ray / voe lee oh / sh end are ay.

When is the next bus back to Florence?
Quando parte il prossimo autobus per Firenze?
Coo an doe / part ay / eel / pro see mo / auto boos / pair / Fee wren zee?

Is there any other way I can get to Florence?
C'è un altro modo per andare a Firenze?
Chay / oon / altro / mode oh / pair / and ah ray / ah / Fee wren zay?

By Gondola *Per Gondola* **Pair / Gondola**

I feel sick.
Mi sento male.
Mee / sento / mah lay.

I can't swim.
Non so nuotare.
Non / so / noo oh tar ay.

Have you got a life jacket?
Avete un giubotto salvagente?
Avay tay / oon / gee you boto / salve ah gent ay?

Can I have a go with that pole?
Posso provare il remo della gondola?
Poss oh / pro vah ray / eel / ray mo / della / gone dollar.

Man overboard!
Uomo in mare!
Ooh oh mo / in / mah ray!

Sorry, I didn't think the jetty was so close.
Mi dispiace, non pensavo che il molo fosse cosí vicino.

Mee / dees pee ah chay, / non / pens ah voe / kay / eel / moll low / foss say / co see / vee see no.

Do you think it has sunk right down to the bottom?
Pensi che sia affondato fino al fondo?
Pen see / kay / see ah / ah fond ah toe / fee no / al / fond oh?

By Train   *Per Treno*   **Pair / Tren oh**

Station   *Stazione*   **Stat zee oh nay**
Destination   *Destinazione*   **Dest tea nat zee oh knee**
Platform   *Binario*   **Bin ah ree oh**

There are various types of Italian trains:

Locale   **Low car lay**   Stops at every station
Espresso   **Ess presso**   Doesn't stop at your station
Rapido   **Ra pee doe**   Only stops at the terminal
Super rapido   **Sue pair / ra pee doe**   Doesn't stop at all

What time are the train departures for Verona?
A che ora partono i treni per Verona?
Ah / kay / aura / part toe no / ee / tren knee / pair / Verona?

One ticket for Padua.
Un biglietto per Padova.
Oon / billy et toe / pair / Pad oh va.

Two return tickets to Mantua.
Due biglietti andata e ritorno per Mantova.
Doo ay / billy et tea / and ah ta / ay / ree torn oh / pair / Mun toe va.

Does this train stop at many stations?
Questo treno si ferma a molte stazioni?
Coo es toe / tren oh / see / fair ma / ah / moll tay / sta zee oh knee?

Which platform for Reggio?
Quale binario per Reggio?
Coo ah lay / bean ah rio / pair / Reg jaw?

Do I have to change?
Devo cambiare?
Dev oh / cam bee ah ray?

Does this train stop at Piombino?
Questo treno si ferma a Piombino?
Coo es toe / tren oh / see / fair ma / ah / Pee om bee no.

I wanted to get out at Piombino.
Volevo scendere a Piombino.
Vo lay vo / sen dare ray / ah / Pee om bee no.

Where does this train go to then?
Allora, dove va questo treno?
Ah laura / doe vay / va / coo es toe / tren oh?

I know it's not the right ticket!
Lo so che non è il biglietto giusto!
Low / so / kay / non / ay / eel / billy et toe / juice toe!

How much more?
Quanto ancora?
Coo an toe / an core ah?

Do you accept drachmas?
Può accettare drachmas?
Poo oh / ah chet ah ray / drack muzz?

By Car   *Con L'Auto*   Con L'ow toe

I want to rent a car.
Voglio affittare un auto.
Vo lee oh / aff fee tar ah / oon / ow toe.

Do you have any other colours? My wife does not care for that shade of purple.
Ci sono altri colori? A mia moglie non piace quella tinta di viola.
Chee / so no / al tree / coll law ree? / Ah / mee ah / molly ay / non / pee ah chay / coo ell la / teen ta / dee / vee oh la.

Show me the operating systems (lights – wipers).
Fammi vedere come funziona (luci – tergicristalli).
Far me / ved dare ray / co may / foon zee oh nah / (loo chee – turgy chris tah lee).

What type of petrol does the car consume?
Che tipo di benzina usa la auto?
Kay / tea po / dee / bent seen ah / ooze ah / la / ow toe?

Senza piombo   **Sen za / pee ombo**   Unleaded
Super   **Soup air**   Super
Diesel   **Dee ay zell**   Diesel

Could you fill her up, please?
Mi fa il pieno, per favore?
Me / fah / eel / pee ay no, / pair / fav awe ay?

I would like ten litres.
Vorrei dieci litri.
Vor ay ee / dee ay chee / lee tree.

Give me what you can for this amount of change.
Mi da quello che può per spiccioli.
Mee / da / coo ell oh / kay / poo oh / pair / speach ee oh lee.

Road Rage

Collera di la Strada   Cholera / dee / la / Strah da

Road rage was invented in Italy and without a suitable knowledge of essential expletives you could lose the respect of the traffic police.

Why don't you learn to drive, idiot?
Perchè non impari a guidare, imbecille?
Pair kay / non / eem pa ree / ah / guee dah ray / eem bay seal?

Get out of the way, you dipstick!
Levati da mezzo, buffone!
Lay va tee / da / mets so / boo phone ay!

I didn't know it was a one way street!
Non sapevo che era senso unico!
Non / sap pay vo / kay / air er / senso / ooh knee co!

Who are you hooting at?
A chi suoni cretino?
Ah / key / swan knee / cray teen oh?

I understood that!
Questo l'ho capito!
Coo es toe / lo / cap pee toe!

Here are a choice words to be shouted out of the window at speed, like a true Italian.

Corn ooh toe! *Cornuto!* Bastard! (Literally: Cuckold)

Vay key oh / fee no key oh!
Vecchio finocchio!
Dirty old poofter!

Va / ah / far ray / in / cool oh!
Va a fare in culo!
Go screw yourself!

And the same to you!
Altrettanto!
Al tray tan toe!

Parking *Parcheggio* Par kay jaw

I do not understand the ticket machine instructions.
Non capisco le istruzioni della macchina biglietti.
**Non / cap pees co / lay / east root zee oh knee / dell ah /
mac key na / billy et tee.**

Where do you insert the ticket?
Dove si inserisce il biglietto?
Doe vay / see / in sair ree shay / eel / billy et toe?

The machine does not work.
La macchina non funziona.
La / mac key na / non / foont zee oh na.

The barrier will not go up.
La sbarra non va su.
La / zbar rah / non / va / sue.

I cannot find my car.
Non trovo la mia macchina.
Non / trow vo / la / mee ah / ma key na.

I don't remember the number.
Non mi ricordo il numero.
Non / mee / reek cord doe / eel / noo may roe.

I will know it when I see it.
Lo saprò quando la vedrò.
Low / sap roe / coo an doe / low / ved roe.

I gave a lift to two nuns from Spezia who are in the back seat.
Ho dato un passaggio a due suore di Spezia che sono sul sedile posteriore.
Oh / dah toe / oon / pass ah jaw / ah / doo ay / swore ray / dee / Speh zee ah / kay / so no / sool / said deal lay / poss tay ree or ray.

Car Trouble *Problemi di macchina*

The keys are locked inside the car.
Le chiavi sono chiuse nella macchina.
Lay / key are vee / so no / key ooze ay / nella / ma key na.

I have run out of petrol.
Sono senza benzina.
So no / senza / bent seen ah.

Where is the nearest garage for repairs?
Dov'é l'autorimessa più vicina?
Doe vay / ay / eel / ow toe ree mess ah / pee you / vee chee na?

I have a puncture – engine trouble.
Ho una ruota bucata – problemi con il motore.
Oh / ooh na / boo cat tah – problem mee / con / eel / mow tore ray.

It won't start.
Non parte.
Non / party.

How long will it take?
Quanto tempo ci vorrà?
Coo an toe / tempo / chee / vor ah?

How long?!
Quanto?!
Coo an toe?!

Can't you do it quicker than that?
Non è possibile farlo più velocemente di questo?
Non / ay / poss see bee lay / far low / pee you / vel oh say meant ay / dee / coo ess toe?

Are you sure this is correct? My car is not a Lamborghini.
Siete sicuri che questo è giusto? La mia macchina non è un Lamborghini.
See ate ay / see coo ree / kay / coo es toe / ay / juice toe? / La / mee ah /ow toe / non / ay / oon / Lamborghini.

Where can I hire a motor scooter?
Dove posso affitare un motorino?
Doe vay / posso / ah fee tar ray / oon / mow tore ee no?

Getting Something to Eat and Drink

Fast Food   *Fast Food*   Fast Food

Snack	*Spuntino*	**Spoon tee no**
Drinks	*Bevande*	**Bay van day**
Orange drink	*Aranciata*	**Aran chee ah ta**
Lemonade	*Limonata*	**Lee mo nah ta**

Ice Cream	*Gelato*	**Gell ah toe**
Milk Shake	*Frullato*	**Froo la toe**

Strawberry – chocolate – vanilla – flavour.
Fragola – cioccolato vaniglia – sapore.
Frag oh la – chee ock oh lah toe – van knee lee ah – sap awe ray.

I would like …
Vorrei …
Vor ray …

Strong black coffee	*Espresso*	**Espresso**
Strong, large coffee	*Lungo*	**Loon go**
Coffee with a dash of milk	*Macchiato*	**Ma chee ah toe**
Milk with a dash of coffee	*Caffelatte*	**Café lah tay**
Frothy milky coffee	*Cappuccino*	**Cap poo chee no**

Tea with lemon.
Te con lemone.
Tay / con / lee moan ay.

Tea with cold milk (state cold milk, or you may get it boiled).
Te con latte freddo.
Tay / con / lah tay / fray doe.

A cup of hot chocolate.
Una tazza di cioccolato caldo.
Oo na / tazza / dee / chee ock oh lah toe / cal doe.

Could I have more sugar?
Mi da più zucchero per favore?
Mee da / pee you / zoo kay roe / pair / fav awe ray?

A sandwich: ham; cheese; chicken; salami, tuna; smoked salmon.
Un panino: prosciutto; pollo; formaggio; salame; tonno; salmone affumicato.
Oon / pa knee no: pro chute toe; form ah jaw; pol oh; salami, tone oh; sal mon ay; aff ooh me cat oh.

Essential Questions to Waiters

Waiter   *Cameriere* **Cam air ree ray**
Waitress *Cameriera* **Cam air ree ray**

Could you recommend a good local wine?
Mi può raccomandare un buon vino locale?
Mee / poo oh / rack oh man dah ray / oon / boo on / vee no / low car la?

A glass of red – white wine.
Un bicchiere di vino rosso – di vino bianco.
Oon / bee chee airy / dee / vee no / rosso – dee / vee no / bee an co.

Dry *Secco* **Seck oh**
Not too dry *Non troppo secco* **Non / trop po / seck oh**
Very dry *Molto secco* **Moll toe / seck oh**
Semi sweet *Semi dolce* **Sam me / doll chay**
Sweet *Dolce* **Doll chay**
Rich and fruity *Ricco e fruttato* **Rick co / ay / fruit tah toe**

Mineral water – sparkling – still.
Acqua minerale – con gas – senza gas.
Aqua / meaner ah lay – con gas – senza gas.

I'll have a beer please.
Una birra per favore.
Oon ah / beer ah / pair / fav awe ray.

The bill please.
Il conto, per favore.
Eel / con toe / pair / fav awe ray.

There seems to be a mistake.
Mi sembra che c'è un errore.
Mee / sem bra / chay / oon / air awe ray.

Is the tip included?
E' compreso il servizio?
Ay / com press oh / eel / sair vee zee oh?

I do not think it is necessary to raise your voice like that. I only asked.
Non è necessario alzare la voce. Era solo una piccola domanda.
**Non / ay / ne chess are ee oh / alt sah ray / la / voe chay.
Air ah / solo / oon ah / pee cola / demand oh**.

Slow Food

Breakfast	*Prima colazione*	**Prima / cola zee oh nay**
Lunch	*Colazione*	**Cola zee oh nay**
Dinner	*Pranzo*	**Prune zo**
Supper	*Cena*	**Chay na**

Antipasto	Starters	**Anti past toe**
Minestrone	Soup	**Mee nay strow nay**
Pesce	Fish	**Pay shay**
Carne	Meat	**Car nay**
Legumi	Vegetable	**Lay goo me**
Formaggio	Cheese	**For ma jaw**
Dessert	Dessert	**Dess air**

As pasta is the national dish, it is as well to be clear about a few of them:

Bucatini **Boo car tee nee** spaghetti with a hole
Conchiglia **Con key lee ah** shell-shaped pasta
Farfalle **Far fah lay** butterfly-shaped pasta
Fettuccine **Fet too chee nay** flattened spaghetti
Fusilli **Foo silly** short spiral pasta pieces
Gnocchi **Knee ock key** small parcels made with potato flour
Penne **Pen nay** large macaroni with a bias cut
Totelloni **Tort tell oh nay** round, stuffed pasta

I will have penne with a tomato and mozzarella salad.
Prendero' delle penne e una insalata di pomodori e mozzarella.
Pram day roh/ dell lay / pen nay / ay / oon ah / inn sal ah ta / dee / pom oh door ee/ ay / mot sar ella.

I am still waiting for my order.
Sto ancora aspettando la mia ordinazione.
Stock / and core ay / aspect and oh / lah / mee ah / or din ah zee oh nay.

You didn't say the penne were finished.
Non ha detto che erano terminate le penne.
Non / ah / debt toe / kay / air ah no / tare mee na toe / lay / pen nay.

Could I see the menu again?
Posso rivedere il menu?
Poss so / reev ah dare ray / eel / menu ?

What do you mean it's too late to order anything else?
Cosa significa è troppo tardi per ordinare qualcosa altro?
Cosa / seen knee fee car / ay / trop po / tardy / pair / or dinar ray / coo al cosa / ultro?

Getting a Bed

Five Star
There should be no need to speak Italian in a five star hotel. Receptionists, head waiters, waiters, barmen, bell-boys and chambermaids speak English.

Four Star
There should be no need to speak Italian in a four star hotel. Receptionists, head waiters, and barmen will love to speak English.

Three Star
There should be no need to speak Italian in a three star hotel. The receptionist and head waiter will speak English fluently. Other members of the staff will think they speak it fluently.

Two Star
The receptionist may be under the impression that he or she speaks English, but in fact is quite unintelligible. Persevere.

Do you have a room for one night?
Avete una stanza per una notte?
Ah vay tay / ooh na / stanza / pair / oon ah / knot ay?

I would like a room with a double bed.
Desidero una camera con letto matrimoniale.
Des see dare oh / oon ah / camera / con / let toe / mat ree moan ee ah lay.

At what time do you stop serving breakfast?
Fino a che ora si prende la prima colazione?
Fee no / ah / kay / aura / see / pren day / la / pree ma / coll at zee oh nay?

One Star
The owner manager will welcome you with open arms, hugs and kisses, speak to you in Spaghetti Western American, and try to diddle you.

What are these charges for?
Per che cosa sono questi extra sul mio conto?
Pair / kay / cosa / so no / coo es tee / extra / sool / mee oh / con toe?

But there are no phones in your rooms, and I have a mobile anyway.
Ma non ci sono telefoni nelle vostre stanze, è ho un telefono cellulare.
Ma / non / chee / so no / telephone knee / nell ay / voss tray / stan zay / ay / oh / oon / telephone oh / cell loo la ray.

There is no light bulb in my bedroom.
Manca la lampadina nella mia camera.
Monk ah / la / lamp ah dean ah / nella / mee ah / cam air ah.

There is no toilet paper in my bathroom.
Non c'è carta igienica nel bagno.
Non / chay / carter / ee gee en nicker / nell / bun yo.

Excuse me, but there's a horse's head in my bed.
Mi scusi, ma c'è una testa di cavallo nel mio letto.
Me / skoo zee / ma / chay / oon ah / testa / dee / cav ah yo / nell / me oh / let toe.

No Star

This will be a pension. The owner-manager won't understand a word you say whether or not you use this book, but try:

Is the water traditionally rusty in this area?
L'acqua normalmente rugginosa in questa regione?
Lack ooh ah / normal meant ay / roo gee nose ah / in / coo ess tee / ray jaw nay?

Is there a lavatory on the same floor or is it at the bottom of the garden?
C'è un bagno sullo stesso piano, o giù nel giardino?
Chay / oon / ban ee oh / sue low / stess oh / piano / oh / gee you / nell / gee are dee no?

Does your wife only practise opera arias at night?
Sua moglie pratica il canto d'opera di notte?
Sue ah / molly ay / prack tee ka / eel / canto / doe pair ah / dee / not tay?

Will the girls in high heels be going up and down the stairs all night?
Le ragazze con i tacchi alti vanno su tutta la notte?
Lay / rag gut say / con / tacky / al tea / vun no / sue / toot ah / la / knot ay?

Getting Service

At the Bookshop; Newsagent

In Libreria; Edicola **In / Leeb rare ree ah; / Eddy cola**

Do you have any local guide books in English?
Avete delle guide sulla località in inglese?
Ah vay tay / day lay / goo ee day / sue la / lock ally ta / in / in glaze ay?

Have you any maps of the town and district?
Avete della mappe della città è dintorni?
Ah vay tay / del lay / map pay / de lay / cheater / ay / dean tore knee?

Do you have any cheap lighters?
Avete degli accendini economici?
Ah vay tay / daily / ah send dee knee / echo nom mee chee?

Do you have any English newspapers?
Avete dei giornali in inglese?
Ah vay tay / day yee / gee or na lee / in / in glaze ay?

Do you have any nudie magazines?
Avete delle riviste pornografiche?
Ah vay tay / del lay / reeve east tay / pornograph fee kay?

I wasn't trying to steal it, I just didn't want my wife to know I was buying it.
Non cercavo di rubarlo, non volevo far sapere a mia moglie che lo compravo.
Non / sair ka vo / dee / roo bar low, / non / vol lay vo / far / sap air ray / ay / mee ah / molly ay / kay / low / comp rah vo.

At the Post Office

All l'ufficio Postale **Al / loo fee chee oh / Post ah lay**

Locale = local; *Città* = City; *Estero* = Aboard

How much is a stamp for …?
Quanto costa un francobollo per questo …?
Coo an toe / cost ah / oon / franco bollo / pair …?

I would like to register this parcel.
Vorrei mandare questo pacchetto per raccomandata.
Vor ray / mun dah ray / coo es toe / packet toe / pair / rack command ah ta.

Which window do I go to then?
Quale sportello?
Coo ah lay / sport tell oh?

I have just been there and they told me to come here!
Sono appena stato al'altro sportello e mi hanno detto di venire qui!
Sono / ah pay na / stat oh / al / altro / sport tell oh / ay / mee / anno / debt toe / dee / ven ee ray / key!

This parcel is fragile. Please be careful.
Questo pacco è fragile. Attenzione per favore.
Coo es toe / pack oh / ay / fraj eel. / At tent zee oh nay / pair / fav awe ray.

It wasn't leaking before I handed it to you.
Non colavava prima di averlo consegnato a lei.
Non / coll lava / pree ma / dee / av air low / con say knee ah toe / ah / lay yee.

Could I have it back please.
Me lo da indietro per favore.
May / low / da / in dee ay tro / pair / fav awe ray.

38

At the Bank   *In Banca*   In / Bunker

The cash point has swallowed my card.
La macchina ha ritenuto la mia carta di credito.
La / ma key na / ah / ree ten ooh toe / la / mee ah / carter / dee / credit oh.

It worked yesterday.
Funzionava ieri.
Foont see oh na vah / ee air ee.

No, I have not spent my limit for today.
No, non ho speso il mio limite per oggi.
No, / non / oh / spay zo / eel / me oh / lee meet ay / pair / oj gee.

Then could you change these travellers cheques?
Mi può cambiare questi travellers cheques?
Mee / poo oh / come bee are ray / coo ess tee / travellers cheques?

What is the rate of exchange?
Qual'è il corso del cambio?
Coo al ay / eel / caw sew / del / cam bee oh?

I would like to see the manager.
Vorrei parlare col direttore.
Vor ray yee / pa lah ray / col / dee rhett tore ray.

Could I ring my bank at home?
Posso telefonare alla mia banca?
Posso / telephone are ay / al lah / mee ah / bunker?

Where do I sign?
Dove firmo?
Doe vay / feer mo?

At the Hairstylist

Dal Parruchiere   Dal / Pa roo key air ray

Cosa / lay / pee ah chair ebb bay?
Cosa le piacerebbe?
What would you like?

For her:

Shampoo and blow dry please.
Shampoo è asciugatura per favore.
Shampoo / ay / ah sugar too rah / pair / fav awe ray.

Could you just trim it a little?
Mi può tagliare solo un poco?
Me / poo oh / tally ah ray / solo / oon / poke oh?

I'd like to have my hair streaked.
Vorrei farmi le mèches.
Vor ray / farm mee / lay / mesh.

Blonde – brunette – auburn – silver – green
Biondo – bruno – castano – argento – verde.
Beyond oh – bruno – cast ah knee oh – are jent toe – vair day.

But I didn't want it cut at all!
Ma, non volevo un taglio!
Ma, / non / vo lay vo / oon / tally oh!

For him:

I want it short.
Li voglio corti.
Lee / voe lee oh / core tea.

Not too short.
Non troppo corti.
Non / trop po / core tea.

A little bit off the sides.
Un poco ai lati.
Oon / poke oh / ay / lah tea.

Were you trained as a hairdresser in the army?
Ha imparato il mestiere nell' esercito?
Ah / eem par ah toe / eel / mess tea air ay / nell / ay sair chee toe?

Having Fun *Divertimento* Dee vert tea men toe

Sight Seeing

Visita ai Monumenti Vee see ta / ay / monument tea

At what time can one tour the gallery – basilica?
A che ora apre la galleria – basilica?
Ah / kay / aura / ah pray / la / gal air ee ah – basilica?

My feet are killing me. I'm going to sit in the pews and pretend I'm praying.
Miei piedi mi ammazzano. Mi vado a sedere nel banco, facendo finta di pregare.
Mee ay ee / pee ay dee / mee / am marts ah no. / Mee / vah doe / ah / said air ah / nell / banco, / fah chen doe / feen tah / dee / preg ah ray.

Is the water in the font drinkable?
L'acqua della fontana è potabile?
Lack coo ah / della / font ah nah / ay / pot ah bee lay?

Yes, the ceiling is beautiful, but I've got a crick in my neck.
Si', il soffito è bellissimo, ma mi è venuto il torcicollo.
See, / eel / so fee toe / ay / bell lee see mo, / ma / me / ay ven ooh toe / eel / torch ee coll oh.

I don't wish to be irreverent, but are there any toilets for tourists in this cathedral?
Non vorrei essere irriverente, ma ci sono toilets per turisti in questa cattedrale?
Non / vor ray / ess ay ray / ee ray vay rent ay, / ma / chee / sono / too a lets / pair / too ree stee / in / coo ess ta / cat aid rah lay?

This is the 23rd church I've visited this morning. Are there any cinemas?
Questa è la ventitreesima chiesa che ho visitato sta mattina. Ci sono cinema?
Coo esta / ah / la / vent tee ree see ma / key ess ah / kay / oh / vee zee ta toe / sta / mat tina? Chee / so no / see nay ma?

How deep do the catacombs go? I feel claustophobic.
Quanto profondo sono le catacombe? Mi sento claustrofobico.
**Coo aunt oh / pro fond oh / so no / lay / catacomb bay? /
Mee / sent oh / claustro phobic oh**.

Now I've seen Naples, what happens?
Ora che ho visitato Napoli, che succede?
**Aura / kay / oh / vee see ta toe / Nap po lee / kay / sook
say day?**

A Day Trip to Sicily

Una Giornata in sicilia
Oon ah / Gee or nah ta / in / see chilly ah

The door was open. I was being curious.
La porta era aperta, ero curiouso.
La / port ah / air ah / up air tah, / air oh / coo ree oh so.

Please don't shoot.
Si prega di non sparare.
See / pray ga / dee / non / spa rare ray.

I have my hands up.
Ho le mani in altro.
Oh lay / ma knee / in / ultro.

I am on my knees.
Sono in ginocchio.
So no / in / gee knock ee oh.

My great great grandfather was from Palermo.
Mio bis bisnonno è nato a Palermo.
**Mee oh / bees / bees non oh / ay / nah toe / ah / Pal air
mo**.

At the Carnival in Venice

Al Carnevale di venezia
Al / Carnival lay / dee / vein net zee ah

I love your mask. Take it off and I'll give you a kiss.
Quarto mi piace tua maschera. Se lo togli, ti bacerò.
Coo are toe / mee / pee ah chay / too ah / musk air ah. /
Say / low / toll yee, / tea / batch air roe.

Aren't you Doris?
Sei Doris?
Say Doris?

Who are you then?
Ma chi sei?
Ma / key say?

I'm frightfully sorry, sir.
Mi scusi profondamente, Signore.
Mee / skoo see / prof fond ah men tay, / Seen your ay.

At the Opera   *All'Opera*   **Al / Oh pair ah**

Box Office *Biglietteria* **Billy et air ee ah**
Stalls *Poltrone in platea* **Poll trone ay / in / plat tay ah**
Circle   *Prima galleria* **Prima / gallery ee ah**
Gods   *Palco*   **Pal co**

Open air theatre *Teatro all aperto* **Tay ah tro / al / ah pair toe**

I would like a seat – two seats – for tonight.
Vorrei una poltrona – due poltrone – per stasera.
Vor ray ee / oon ah / poll trone ah – doo ay / pol trow knee – pair / stass air ah.

When does the perfomance finish?
Quando finisce lo spettacolo?
Coo an doe / finish ay / lo / speck tack oh lo?

Give me a programme please.
Mi da un programma per favore.
Mee / da / oon / programme ah / pair / fav awe ray.

This is not the opera I booked tickets for.
Questa non è l'opera per la quale ho prenotato i biglietti.
Coo est ah / non / ay / lo pair ah / pair / lah / coo ah lay / oh / pren oh tar toe / ee / billy et tea.

On the Beach *Sulla Spiaggia* Sue la / Spee ah gee ah

What you may hear:

Eye / vees toe! *Hai visto!* Wow! Look!
Bell ay / tettay! *Belle tette!* Nice tits!
Bell / cool oh! *Bel culo!* Great arse!

Where is the nudist beach?
Dove è la spiaggia nudista.
Do vay / la / spee ah gee ah / noo dee star.

I would like a beach umbrella.
Vorrei un ombrellone.
Vor ray ee / oon / om bray oh knee.

And under it a beach bed.
E un lettino a sdraio sotto.
Ay / oon / let tea no / ay / sdra yee oh / sotto.

Are there jellyfish in the sea?
Ci sono meduse nel mare?
Chee / so no / med ooze ay / nel / mah ray?

45

Could your children play somewhere else?
I bambini possono giocare da qualche altra parte?
Ee / bambini / poss oh no / jaw car ay / da / coo al chay / ultra / part ay?

How many speeds are there on this water scooter/jet ski?
Quante velocità ci sono sulla moto d'acqua?
Coo aunt ay / velo cheat ah / chee / sue la / mow toe / da aqua?

Of course I've driven one before.
Naturalmente ne ho guidato uno nel passato.
Natural ah men tay / nay / oh / goo ee da toe / oon oh / nell / pass ah toe.

I assure you, the speed boat came from nowhere.
Le assicuro, il motoscafo è venuto da non so dove.
Lay / ass see coo roe / eel / mow toe scarf oh / ay / ven ooh toe / da / non / so / doe vay.

At the Swimming Pool   *In Piscina*   In Pee sheen ah

Which is the deep end?
Dovè la parte più profonda?
Doe vay / la / part ay / pee you / mass / pro fond ah?

You were wrong.
Ha sbagliato.
Ah / sbully are toe.

Don't worry, I will be fine in a few days.
Non ti preocupare, starò benissimo fra qualche giorno.
Non / tee / pray oh coo pa ray / star oh / ben knee see mo / fra / coo al kay / jaw no.

At the Disco   *In Disco*   in / Disco

What did you say?
Cosa mi hai detto?
Coze ah / mee / eye / debt toe?

Sorry, I can't hear a thing.
Scusa, non sento niente.
Scusa, / non / sent toe / knee en tay.

At the Club   *Al Club*   Al / Club

For Boys: *Per Ragazzi*   **Pair / Rag gut see**

Saw you on the beach today.
Oggi ti ho visto sulla spiaggia.
Odd gee / tee / oh / vees toe / sue la / spee ah gee ah.

Do you come here often?
Vieni qui spesso?
Vee en ee / key / spess oh?

Does your brother always accompany you?
Tuo fratello ti accompagna sempre?
Too oh / frat ell oh / tee / ack company knee ah / sem pray?

Is there any way we can get rid of him?
C'è qualche modo per sganciarlo?
Say / coo al kay / mow doe / pair / skun chee are low?

Give us a kiss.
Dammi un bacio.
Dummy / oon / batch ee oh.

For Girls: *Per Ragazze* **Pàir / Rag gut say**

No, I am not alone. I am with another girl.
No, non sono solo. Sto in compagnia di una ragazza.
No, / non / so no / solo. / Stow / in / com pa knee ah / dee / ooh na / rag guts sa.

She has a boy friend.
Lei ha un fidanzato.
Lay ee / ah / oon / feed anne's ah toe.

The big one with the bald head and tattoos.
Quello grande senza capelli è con tatuaggi.
Coo el oh / grand day / sent za / cap elly / ay / con / tattoo ah gee.

I think it's a bit too soon for that.
Penso che è un po' presto anche per questo.
Pen so / kay / ay / oon / poh / press toe / anne kay / pair / coo ess toe.

At the Gymn *In Palestra* **In / Palace tra**

I would like a massage and sauna to follow.
Vorrei un massaggio e una sauna dopo.
Vor ay ee / oon / mass sarge jaw / ay / ooh na / sauna / dop po.

How much is it for each one?
Quanto costa ognuno?
Coo an toe / costa / on yawn oh?

That is too hard – too soft.
Questo è troppo duro – troppo morbido.
Coo ess toe / ay / trop po / due roe – trop po / morbid oh.

48

Can you do that again?
Puoi farcelo di nuovo?
Poo oh ee / far chello / dee / noo oh vo?

Shopping   *Spese*   **Spays zay**

I would like that.
Mi piacerebbe quello.
Mee / pee ah chay reb bay / coo ell oh.

What does this cost?
Quanto costa questo?
Coo an toe / costa / coo ess toe?

That's outrageous!
Questo è carissimo!
Coo ess toe / ay / car ree see mo!

Is that the best you can do?
E il meglio che può fare?
Ay / eel / melly oh / kay / poo oh / far ray?

It is still too expensive.
E sempre troppo caro.
Ay / sem pray / trop po / car roe.

I'll take it.
Lo compro.
Lo / com pro.

I'll leave it.
Lo lascio.
Lo / lash she oh.

I was here before, and I want to buy the Venetian goblet after all.
Sono venuto prima è voglio la coppa veneziana dopotutto.
So no / ven ooh toe / pree ma / ay / voe lee oh / la / copper / ven net zee ah na / doppo toot oh.

Oh dear, I've dropped it.
Momma mia, l'ho lasciato cadere.
Mama / me ah, / lo / lash ee ah toe / cad air ray.

Are you insured for damages?
Siete assicurati per danni?
See et ay / ass see coo rat tea / pair / dah knee?

No, I can't afford another one.
No, non posso permettermi un altro.
No / non / poss oh / pair met air mee / oon / altro.

What day is the street market?
Quando c'è il mercato?
Coo an doe / kay / eel / mare car toe?

At the Boutique *Alla Boutique* Al lah / boo teak

I bought this last week and would like to exchange it.
*Ho comprato questo la settimana scorsa è non mi va bene.
Me lo può cambiare?*
**Oh / com pra toe / coo ess toe / la / settee mah nah /
score sa / ay / non / mee / va / ben nay. / Mee / lo / poo
oh / come bee are ray?**

I don't like the colour.
Non mi piace il colore.
Non / mee / pee ah chay / eel / coll law ray.

It doesn't fit me.
Questo non mi sta bene.
Coo ess toe / non / mee / star / ben nay.

It is: too big; too small; too wide; too tight.
*E: troppo grande; troppo piccolo; troppo largo; troppo
stretto.*
**Ay: trop po / grand ay; trop po / peek oh low; trop po /
lah go; trop po / stret toe.**

May I try these shoes on?
Posso provare queste scarpe?
Posso / pro vah ray /coo ess tay / scar pay?

Could you help me? I can't get them off.
Mi può aiutare? Non posso togliermeli.
**Mee / pee oh / eye you tar ray? / Non / posso / tolly air
melly.**

Do you sell crutches?
Vendete grucce?
Vend day tay / grew chay?

At the Sex Shop   *Nil Sex Shop*   Nil Sex Shop

I am not too fond of that pink. Do you have them in black?
Non mi piace il rosa. Li aveti in nero?
Non / me / pee a chay / eel / rosa / lee / av ah tea / in / nay roe?

Is there a book of instructions?
C'è un libro di istruzioni?
Say / oon / lee bro / dee / ees true zee oh nay?

Please include the right batteries.
Per favore includa le batterie per questo.
Per / fav or ay / in cloo da / lay / bat er ree ah / pair / coo ess toe.

Sex   *Sex*   Sex

Mature female to Toy Boy:

I love that simmering look of desire in your eyes. Is it for me?
Quanto amo quel profondo sguardo di desiderio nei tuoi occhi. E per me?
Coo aunt toe / amo / coo ell / pro fond oh / skoo are doe / dee / des see dare ee oh / nay ee / too ee oh / ock key. / Ay / pair / may?

Do you work out or is that your natural build?
Fai la ginnastica o tua forma è così naturalmente?
Fye / la / gin ass ticker / oh / too ah / form ah / ay / cosy / natural men tay?

Have you finished?
Hai finito?
Eye / fee knee toe?

So soon?
Cosi presto?
Cosy / press toe?

Sugar Daddy to Nymphette:

Hallo my dear. Can I buy you an ice cream – glass of wine –
bottle of vodka?
*Ciao cara. Ti posso comprare un gelato – un bicchiere di
vino – una bottiglia di vodka?*
**Chow / cara / tee / poss oh / com pra ray / oon / gell ah
toe – oon / bee chee air ee / dee / vee no – oon ah / botty
lee ah / dee / vodka.**

Are you on the pill?
Prendi la pillola?
Pren dee / la / pill oh lah?

Won't be a minute. I'll just get my viagra.
Aspetta un minuto. Prendo mio viagra.
**Ass pet ah / oon / mean ooh toe. / Pren doe / me oh / vee
agra.**

Young Stud to Bimbo:

Are you from around here?
Di dove sei?
Dee / doe vay / say ee?

Like to show me your little chapel?
Mi fa vedere la sua piccola cappella?
Mee / fa / vay dare ray / la / sewer / cap ella?

All right, darling?
Va bene, cara?
Va / ben nay, / cara?

For Both:

What do you think you are doing?
Che cosa stai facendo?
Kay / coze ah / sty / fah chen do?

Leave me alone.
Lasciami in pace.
Lash ee ah mee / in / pa chay.

I don't fancy you.
Tu non mi piaci.
Two / non / mee / pee ah chee.

I have a dangerously virulent venereal disease.
Ho una pericolosa malattia virulenta venerea.
Oh / oon ah / perry co low sah / ma la tea ah / vee roo lent ta / ven air ree ah.

At the Police

Al Posto di Polizia   **Al / Posto / dee / Pol eat zee ah**

Italian law enforcement officers come in three sizes with four names. The Guardior or Vigili, who are only more or less active in the towns, the Carabinieri, who are more or less active in town and country, and the Metropolitani, who only pretend to be active in Rome. Most Italian police are tourist friendly, especially if you are a shapely blonde. If not, use the following phrase at all times:

Non capisco niente.
Non / cap pees coe / knee en tay.
I don't understand a thing.

However, if you get into trouble and want to find the police then look for the street sign 'PS' or ask for the 'Questura' **Coo ess too rah**. The following may help.

My car has been broken into and they have stolen my:
Sono entrati nella mia macchina è mi hanno robato:
So no / en trah tee / nella / mee ah / mack key na / ay / mee / anno / rob ah toe:

Luggage	*Bagagli*	**Bug ah lee**
Briefcase	*Cartella*	**Cart ella**
Laptop	*Computer portatile*	**Computer / port ah tea lay**

My sixteen year old daughter.
Mia figlia di sedici anni.
Mee ah / fee lee ah / dee / said ee chee / annie.

I have been mugged and they have taken my:
Mi hanno derubato, hanno preso:
Mee / anno / de roo bar toe / anno / press oh:

Bag	*Borsa*	**Bore sa**
Wallet	*Porta foglio*	**Port ah / folly oh**
Credit cards	*Carte de credito*	**Cart ay / dee / cred dee toe**
Passport	*Passaporto*	**Pass ah port toe**
Rolex watch	*Orologio Rolex*	**Oro lodge jaw / Rolex**
Plane ticket	*Biglietto di aereo*	**Billy et toe / dee / air ee oh**
Wedding ring	*Fede nuziale*	**Fed day / noo zee ah lay**

One million in cash.
Un milione in biglietti di banca.
Oon / meal lee oh nay / in / billy et toe / dee / bunker.

Everything I have in the whole wide world.
Tutto quello che ho nel mondo.
Toot oh / coo ell oh / kay / oh / nell / mon doe.

If you are arrested for a minor misdemeanor, ask for the nearest Consulate (closed at week-ends) thus:

I wish to speak to the Ambassador who is a personal friend of mine.
Desidero parlare con l'ambasciatore che è mio buon amico.
Des ee day row / par lah ray / con / lamba ski ah tore ay / kay / ay / me oh / boo on / am eek oh.

And casually drop a wad of notes on the floor.

Public Notices You May Come Up Against

CHIUSO	Closed
APERTO	Open
INFORMAZIONE	Information
ASCENSORE	Lift/Elevator
NON USCIRE	No Exit
NON ENTRARE	No Entry
NON FUMARE	No Smoking
VIETATO NUOTARE	No Bathing
VIETATO SPUTARE	No Spitting
COMPLETO	No Vacancies
AQUA POTABILE	Drinking Water
SIGNORA	Ladies
SIGNORE	Gentlemen
FUORI SERVIZIO	Out of Order

OCCUPATO	Engaged/Occupied
LIBERO	Free/Vacant
TIRARE	Pull
SPINGERE	Push
SUONARE	Ring (the bell)
ALZARE	Lift/Raise
VERNICE FRESCA	Wet Paint
NON TOCCARE	Do Not Touch
DIVIETO DI SOSTA	No Parking
SENSO UNIVO	One Way Street
PASSAGGIO A LIVELLO	Level Crossing
PASSAGGIO PEDONALE	Pedestrian Crossing
STOP	Stop
PERICOLO	Danger
POMPIERE	Fire Brigade
PRIVATO	Private
VIETATO ENTRARE	Keep Out
ATTENZIONE	Warning
ATTENTI AL CANE	Beware Of The Dog
CHIUSO PER LUTTO	Closed For Mourning

NB: On Italian taps:

'C' stands for *Caldo* which means Hot
'F' stands for *Freddo* which means Cold

Phrases You May Hear

Kay / voo oh lo?
Che vuole?
What do you want?

Devay / pag ah ray / in / anne tee see po.
Deve pagare in anticipo.
You must pay in advance.

Toot ay / lay / stan zay – tav oh lee – so no / ock coo part ay.
Tutte le stanze – tavoli – sono occupate.
All our rooms/tables are taken.

Lay ee / ee / in / ree tar doe.
Lei è in ritardo.
You are too late.

Key / ay / eel / pro see mo?
Chi è il prossimo?
Who is next?

Eel / sue oh / no may / pair / fav awe ray.
Il suo nome per favore.
Your name please.

Ree tore knee / pee you / tar dee.
Ritorni più tardi.
Come back later.

Ass petty / oon / momento.
Aspetti un momento.
Wait a moment.

Non / low / so.
Non lo so.
I don't know.

Non foont zee oh na.
Non funziona.
It doesn't work.

Kay / coze ah / star / far chen doe?
Che cosa sta facendo?
What are you doing?

Coo ess toe / non / ay / pair may so.
Questo non è permesso.
That is not allowed.

Eel / numero / ay / sbah lee ah toe.
Il numero è sbagliato.
You have the wrong number.

Non / lay / poss oh / eye you tar ray.
Non la posso aiutare.
I cannot help you.

Ay / oon / boo on / pets so.
E un buon' pezzo.
It is a very good price.

Non / ay / abba stanza.
Non è abbastanza.
That is not enough.

Eel / sair vee zee oh / non / ay / in clue zo.
Il servizio non è incluso.
Service is not included.

Non / lo / doe man dee / ah / may / so no / anne key oh / oon oh / stran eye roe / coo ee.
Non lo domandi a me, sono anch'io uno straniero qui.
Don't ask me, I am a stranger here myself.

Last Words

I miss you.
Tu mi manchi tanto.
Two / mee / monkey / tun toe.

See you. *Ciao*. **Chee ow**.

It doesn't matter.
Non importa.
Non / import ah.

No, I only speak Italian. I do not understand it.
No, parlo solo italiano. Non lo capisco.
No, / parlo / solo / it ally ah no. / Non / low / cap pees co.

Does anybody here speak English?
C'è qualcuno qui che parla inglese?
Chay / coo al coo no / coo ee / kay / parla / in glaze ay?

Chee ow